bby Practice Pages

Beginning Addition 0-10

by
Debby Head and Libby Pollett

© 2004 bby Publications

SMBSD
CPO

bby
Publications

CONTENTS

Introduction

The purpose of _bby Practice Pages: Beginning Addition 0-10_ is to provide opportunities for young children to practice using a ten-grid to think about addition. These Practice Pages are most effective when used to review previously taught concepts and skills using models explored and practiced in _Number Literacy: Reading and Writing the Language of Numbers_.

Use these Practice Pages to introduce your children to the use of numbers and symbols as a form of communicating the concept of addition. As you do so, your children will grow in their number-sense, number literacy and algebraic thinking.

Children will practice illustrating the solution to an addition fact. Memorization will occur as your children store valuable visual images in their long-term memory banks.

How can using a ten-grid strengthen a child's sense of number?

Because a child's lead into number is through geometry, it only makes sense to use the ten-grid, whose power lies in its simplicity. Its rectangular, symmetrical arrangement makes it an easy tool to use for modeling number relationships. A child who confidently uses the tidiness of the ten-grid will recall an image of the grid and strengthen his/her number sense. Young children will use the ten-grid to make personal connections between numbers, pictures and words. They will also learn to communicate mathematically with pictures.

Children who use the grid develop time-saving shortcuts. Using the ten-grid is more effective than the time-consuming and inefficient method of laboriously drawing scattered tallies or sticks, as shown in the example to the right.

Likewise a young mathematician is often distracted by pictures of animals or objects, as shown here. Such pictures often cause confusion because the young learner is unsure of what to count or becomes distracted by the "cartoon-style" illustrations.

This distraction can be avoided by using color, simple triangles and/or circles placed within a ten-grid.

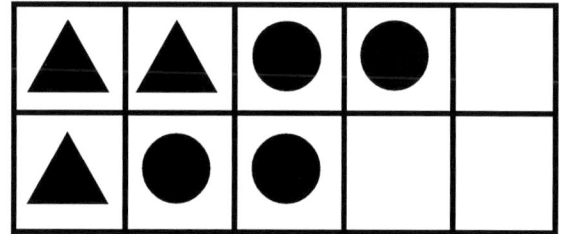

How is this book organized?

bby Practice Pages: Addition Facts 0-10 is separated into four twenty-page sections which are marked with pastel dividers. Each page is divided into six exercises.

Each section is unique in the way opportunities are provided for young mathematicians to personalize the meaning of addition expressions and use a ten-grid to illustrate the solutions. Here is one example from each section.

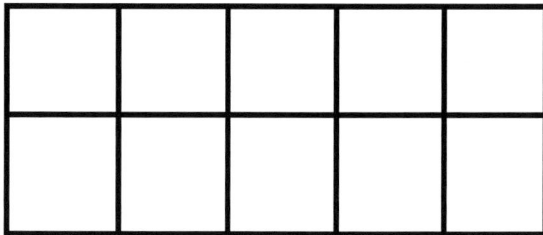

2 green and 3 black

Section One: Use Two Colors

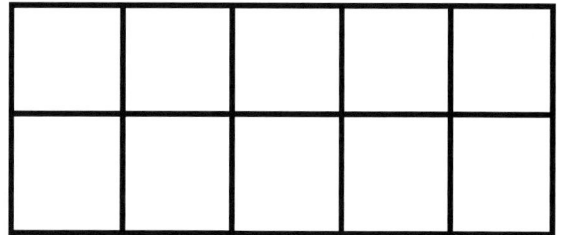

2 green and 3 black

together

Section Two: Use Two Colors. Count the Total. Write the Sum.

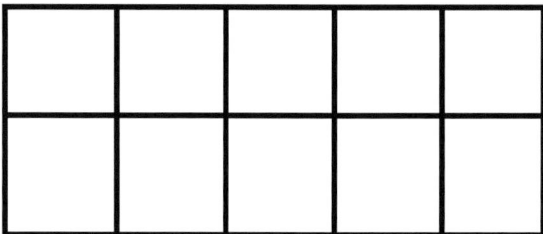

3 + 4 =

green   black

together

Section Three: Solving Horizontal and Vertical Number Sentences Using a Color Word Key

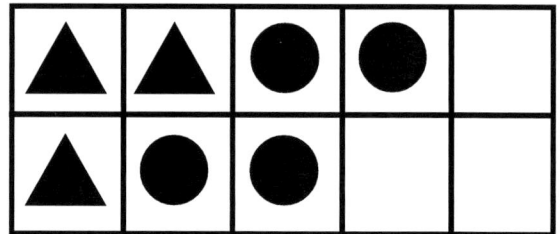

+   =

shapes

Section Four: Writing and Solving Horizontal and Vertical Number Sentences Using a Shape Key

These Practice Pages empower young mathematicians to encode, decode and illustrate addition number sentences by attaching symbolic meaning to the grid model. The position of the grid naturally lends itself to a vertical or horizontal number sentence.

We have discovered that the terms "plus" and "equal" have little meaning to young learners. Therefore, when attempting to read or write an addition number sentence, using such terms can impede understanding. However, this language roadblock can be detoured if those same young learners think about symbols such as:

+ meaning "**put together**"
= meaning "**the same as**"

With maturity, experience and repeated exposure, these same children will begin to use the terms "plus" and "equal" because they understand what is being communicated by the symbols. We have found it helpful to have our children circle the symbols before beginning to illustrate, as a reminder of the meaning of the statement.

How do I incorporate these Practice Pages into my curriculum?
You will find the versatility of these Practice Pages will make them a most valuable tool! Many teachers use them as:
- daily practice and review.
- homework.
- assessments (quizzes, pre-tests, post-tests, etc.).
- a supplement to *Number Literacy: Reading and Writing the Language of Numbers.*

Once you have introduced the ten-grid and the related skills, we recommend daily use. Here's how that might work. Duplicate class sets of your chosen blackline masters. Cut apart along the broken lines that are marked with scissors. Distribute one-sixth of a page each day to each student. You can decide if you want each child to have the same copy or if you want to alternate copies to discourage any little eyes from "borrowing answers". We like to use one section each day, thus spreading out the practice. However, we encourage you to use them to best meet the needs of your children.

How can I help my children develop Big Ideas related to addition?
These Practice Pages provide opportunities for the discovery of Big Ideas such as those related to estimation, reasonableness of an answer, sets and subsets and how to check an answer, to name a few. Because good teaching develops from good questions, we encourage you to ask questions, such as the ones listed below, to stimulate rich mathematical conversations, language and discoveries.

- Do you see more circles or triangles?
- Do you see fewer circles or triangles?
- Do you see an odd or even number of shapes?
- Look at the set of triangles (circles). How many triangles (circles) do you see?
- What number would you write to match the number of triangles (circles) in the set?
- Which crayons do you need?
- How many more shapes do you need to draw to fill the grid?
- Is the number sentence horizontal or vertical?
- Did you color in some or all of the squares?
- How many more squares do you need to color to fill the grid?

- Did you color an odd or even number of squares?
- Are more squares with or without color?
- Are more squares _____ (color A) or _____ (color B)?
- What is the "sum"?
- What does the word "together" mean?
- What will happen when we put the _____ (color A) and _____ (color B) squares together?
- Can you find and loop the symbol (sign) that means "put together"?
- Can you find and loop the symbol (sign) that means "the same as"?
- Can you find and loop the symbol (sign) that means "plus"?
- Can you find and loop the symbol (sign) that means "equals"?
- Can you find and loop the addition symbol (sign)?
- Can you find and loop the equal symbol (sign)?
- What happens when we add the circles and triangles?
- Look at the grid. Does your answer make sense?
- Look at the grid. Do you think the sum will be more or less than_____?
- Look at the grid. Do you think the sum will be _____ (5) or not _____(5)?

How can I help my children make connections between the mathematics on these Practice Pages and the mathematics in their lives?
Practice Pages naturally provide a springboard for individual or class personalization. Make a habit of telling stories to match the examples. Capture the interest of your children by including their names in the stories you tell. Likewise, encourage your children to tell their own stories, as shown in this example.

When do I incorporate these Practice Pages into our daily routine?
Some of the favorite times for using Practice Pages include:
- in the morning as a sponge activity.
- during center rotations.
- anytime as seatwork.
- after PE, lunch, music, computer lab.
- anytime as a break between other activities.

We encourage you to accept each learner's personal stage of development, while continuing to share more efficient ways of counting and modeling.

How do I teach parents to use these Practice Pages at home?
Keep in mind that your children will be taking their completed daily work samples home to share with their families. Also, you may be using these as homework. It is most important that families are familiar with using the ten-grid as a model for thinking about beginning addition. We recommend the following ways to educate parents.
- Family Night - Activities should include demonstrating number concepts on a ten-grid.
- Classroom Website or Newsletter - If you have a class website or newsletter, post examples complete with brief explanations.
- Parent Letter - The following parent letter is one that you may wish to use. You will receive fewer notes and phone calls if you send either a letter of your own or this one with the first homework assignment.

Dear Parent,
We have been using a grid with 10 spaces to practice illustrating the mathematical meaning of addition by combining sets. Sometimes we use colors and sometimes we use shapes. We are also learning to read, write and illustrate addition number sentences. The ten-grid along with the colors and/or shapes helps us "see" what happens when combining sets.

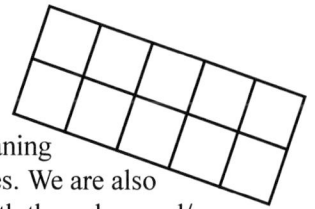

The following are examples of exercises we have been practicing.

Name **Pat**

| 9 | b | b | | |
| 9 | b | | | |

© 2004 bby Publications 502-633-9400

2 green and 3 black

Name **Carole**

| G | G | B | B | B |
| | | | | |

© 2004 bby Publications 502-633-9400

2 green and 3 black

5

together

Name **Martha**

5 red
+ 3 blue

R	B
B	R
R	B
	R
R	

8

together

© 2004 bby Publications 502-633-9400

Name **Elizabeth**

0	●
8	▲
8	

▲	▲
▲	▲
▲	▲
▲	▲

+

shapes

© 2004 bby Publications 502-633-9400

Remember to provide guidance without doing your child's work.

Look for opportunities to practice addition with your child, such as:
- waiting in the doctor's office.
- riding in the car.
- waiting for your order in a restaurant.

Ask your child questions, such as:
- "You have five yellow and two red. Will you fill the ten-grid or will you have some empty spaces?"
- "What combinations of two colors could you use to fill a ten-grid?c
- "I have 6. How many more do I need to have 9?"

4 ▲
+ 1 ●
―――
5

| ▲ | ▲ | ● | | |
| ▲ | ▲ | | | |

4 + 1

When your child is trying to complete an addition number sentence, encourage him/her to think about a ten-grid. By doing so, you will be helping your child become confident when adding.

Please contact me if you have any questions or concerns. Your child and I thank you for your help.

Querido Padre,
Hemos estado usando una cuadrícula con 10 espacios para practicar ilustrando el
significado matemático de la adición al combinar los conjuntos. A veces nosotros usamos
los colores y a veces nosotros usamos las formas. También aprendemos a leer, escribir e ilustrar
las expresiones numéricas de la adición. La diez-cuadrícula junto con los colores y/o formas nos ayuda a
«ver» lo que sucede al combinar los conjuntos.

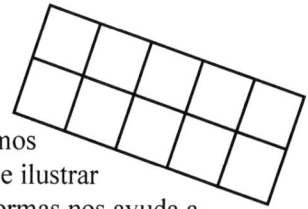

En el siguiente hay los ejemplos de ejercicios que hemos estado practicando.

Name **Pat**

g	b	b		
g	b			

2 green and 3 black

Name **Carole**

G	G	B	B	B

2 green and 3 black

5
together

Name **Martha**

5 red
+ 3 blue

R	B
B	R
R	B
	R
R	

8
together

Name **Elizabeth**

O	●	▲	▲
+ 8	▲	▲	▲
8	shapes	▲	▲

Recuerda, usted puede proporcionar una guía sin hacer el trabajo de su niño.

Practica cuando tiene tiempo extra, como:
- esperando en la oficina de doctor
- va en un coche
- esperando su orden en un restaurante

Pregunta su niño, como:

- "Usted tiene cinco amarillo y dos rojo. ¿Llenará la diez-cuadrícula o tendrá algunos espacios vacíos?"
- "¿Qué combinaciones de dos colores usted puede usar para llenar una diez-cuadrícula?"
- "Tengo 6. ¿Cuántos más necesito a tener 9?"

Cuándo su niño trata de completar una expresión numérica de la adición,
aliéntalo pensar acerca de una diez-cuadrícula. Con esta ayuda, usted
aumentará la confianza de su niño al agregar.

4 ▲
+ 1 ●
——
5

4 + 1

Contácteme por favor si usted tiene cualquiera pregunta o concierne.

Use Two Colors

Here are a few of the ways children have completed the exercises in this section.

Name __Pat__

g	b	b		
g	b			

© 2004 bby Publications 502-633-9400

2 green and 3 black

Name __MIKE__

y	y	y	y	y
r				

© 2004 bby Publications 502-633-9400

1 red and 5 yellow

Name __Cuzétte__

P	P	P	P	B
P	P	P	P	

© 2004 bby Publications 502-633-9400

8 purple and 1 blue

Name __JON__

6 red
and
3 brown

R	B
B	R
R	
B	R
R	R

© 2004 bby Publications 502-633-9400

Name _____

8 purple and 1 blue

6 red
and
3 brown

Name _____

1 red and 5 yellow

10 blue
and
0 black

Name _____

2 green and 3 black

7 brown
and
1 orange

Name _____

bby Practice Pages: **Beginning Addition 0-10**   1

Name _____

8 purple and 0 black

Name _____

8 green and 1 yellow

Name _____

2 red and 3 orange

Name _____

6 black
and
3 yellow

Name _____

3 blue
and
0 purple

Name _____

3 brown
and
6 blue

Name _____

5 purple
and
3 brown

1 green and 6 blue

Name _____

Name _____

2 yellow
and
7 purple

4 orange and 2 red

Name _____

Name _____

8 green
and
2 orange

1 yellow and 8 orange

Name _____

Name _____

2 blue and 6 red

Name _____

3 brown and 2 purple

Name _____

0 black and 6 blue

Name _____

4 purple and 3 blue

Name _____

0 black and 7 green

Name _____

5 brown and 3 orange

4

Name _____

1 orange and 7 black

Name _____

5 green
and
5 red

Name _____

1 green and 6 brown

Name _____

2 orange
and
6 brown

Name _____

10 yellow and 0 blue

Name _____

0 red
and
5 purple

Name _____

1 black and 2 red

© 2004 bby Publications 502-633-9400

Name _____

6 purple and 4 yellow

© 2004 bby Publications 502-633-9400

Name _____

5 yellow and 3 brown

© 2004 bby Publications 502-633-9400

© 2004 bby Publications 502-633-9400

5 red
and
5 blue

Name _____

© 2004 bby Publications 502-633-9400

9 blue
and
1 orange

Name _____

© 2004 bby Publications 502-633-9400

0 brown
and
3 black

Name _____

1 yellow and 9 black

Name _____

0 green and 2 black

Name _____

4 orange and 6 purple

Name _____

3 blue
and
3 green

Name _____

2 brown
and
1 yellow

Name _____

2 purple
and
2 red

Name _____

© 2004 bby Publications 502-633-9400

4 green and 3 purple

3 black
and
1 purple

Name _____

Name _____

© 2004 bby Publications 502-633-9400

5 orange and 4 blue

7 purple
and
2 orange

Name _____

Name _____

© 2004 bby Publications 502-633-9400

8 red and 1 brown

6 yellow
and
2 green

Name _____

Name

2 black and 7 orange

7 blue and 3 brown

Name

5 brown and 0 red

Name

Name

3 orange and 5 green

Name

5 yellow and 1 red

2 purple and 8 green

Name _____

1 brown and 8 green

0 yellow and 4 red

Name _____

5 blue and 2 purple

5 green and 4 blue

Name _____

2 red and 4 black

2 orange and 3 yellow

Name _____

Name

1 red and 7 blue

2 yellow
and
1 purple

Name

Name

3 red and 5 green

4 green
and
1 black

Name

Name

6 red and 4 brown

1 orange
and
3 brown

Name

Name

5 purple and 4 green

6 brown
and
1 orange

Name

Name

3 black and 6 orange

4 blue
and
2 red

Name

Name

3 brown and 7 red

7 yellow
and
1 green

Name

Name

7 red
and
2 yellow

6 yellow and 3 blue

Name

Name

3 orange
and
4 green

2 purple and 5 brown

Name

Name

9 green
and
1 red

3 black and 7 yellow

Name

Name _____

1 black and 1 orange

Name _____

2 orange
and
4 red

Name _____

7 blue and 3 yellow

Name _____

3 yellow
and
4 brown

Name _____

1 brown and 9 blue

Name _____

1 purple
and
5 green

 bby Practice Pages: **Beginning Addition 0-10**

Name

2 black and 8 red

0 green
and
9 blue

Name

Name

2 blue and 2 purple

3 yellow
and
1 black

Name

Name

4 brown and 4 black

1 purple
and
4 orange

Name

bby Practice Pages: **Beginning Addition 0-10**

Name _____

2 orange and 4 blue

Name _____

3 red and 4 orange

Name _____

1 orange and 5 purple

Name _____

4 brown
and
1 green

Name _____

8 purple
and
2 black

Name _____

4 yellow
and
4 orange

 bby Practice Pages: **Beginning Addition 0-10**

Name _____

3 black and 5 blue

Name _____

5 red
and
2 black

Name _____

3 brown and 2 red

Name _____

4 green
and
5 brown

Name _____

4 blue and 6 orange

Name _____

4 purple
and
4 yellow

Name _____

1 black and 4 purple

Name _____

3 brown and 3 yellow

Name _____

6 blue and 1 black

Name _____

6 green
and
2 yellow

Name _____

7 yellow
and
2 red

Name _____

7 purple
and
3 blue

Name

5 orange and 3 yellow

Name

4 red and 5 purple

Name

8 blue and 2 green

Name

3 green
and
6 orange

Name

2 blue
and
3 brown

Name

4 purple
and
1 red

Name _____

3 green and 5 black

Name _____

5 purple
and
2 yellow

Name _____

8 black and 2 brown

Name _____

3 blue
and
6 yellow

Name _____

4 red and 6 green

Name _____

4 brown
and
4 purple

Use Two Colors. Count the Total. Write the Sum.

Here are two ways children have completed the exercises in this section.

Name **Carole**

G	G	B	B	B

2 green and 3 black

5

together

Name **Elvis**

P	P	P	P	B
P	P	P	P	

8 purple and 1 blue

9

together

position on page ▶						
page 21	5	5	5	9	8	9
page 22	10	9	8	7	8	5
page 23	10	4	5	10	9	4
page 24	8	7	10	9	9	7
page 25	10	5	4	3	8	8
page 26	10	6	10	8	9	10
page 27	5	3	4	10	6	2
page 28	10	8	5	10	8	7
page 29	10	9	10	8	7	6
page 30	9	10	8	9	9	6
page 31	5	9	8	7	8	10
page 32	10	9	10	8	5	6
page 33	7	10	8	5	6	7
page 34	6	7	6	6	10	2
page 35	10	6	8	7	9	9
page 36	10	9	5	4	9	7
page 37	6	9	8	4	9	7
page 38	9	8	10	3	3	10
page 39	10	7	8	8	5	7
page 40	6	9	3	9	9	5

Name _____

4 purple and 1 red

together

Name _____

4 red and 5 purple

together

Name _____

2 blue and 3 brown

together

Name _____

5 orange and 3 yellow

together

Name _____

2 green and 3 black

together

Name _____

3 green and 6 orange

together

Name _____

4 purple and 4 yellow

together

Name _____

3 brown and 2 red

together

Name _____

4 green and 5 brown

together

Name _____

3 black and 5 blue

together

Name _____

8 blue and 2 green

together

Name _____

5 red and 2 black

together

Name _____

1 purple and 4 orange

together

Name _____

2 blue and 2 purple

together

Name _____

3 yellow and 1 black

together

Name _____

0 green and 9 blue

together

Name _____

4 blue and 6 orange

together

Name _____

2 black and 8 red

together

Name_____

9 green and 1 red

together

Name_____

2 purple and 5 brown

together

Name_____

3 orange and 4 green

together

Name_____

6 yellow and 3 blue

together

Name_____

4 brown and 4 black

together

Name_____

7 red and 2 yellow

together

Name _____

1 orange and 3 brown

together

Name _____

3 red and 5 green

together

Name _____

4 green and 1 black

together

Name _____

1 red and 7 blue

together

Name _____

3 black and 7 yellow

together

Name _____

2 yellow and 1 purple

together

Name _____

2 purple and 8 green

together

Name _____

7 blue and 3 brown

together

Name _____

5 yellow and 1 red

together

Name _____

2 black and 7 orange

together

Name _____

6 black and 4 brown

together

Name _____

3 orange and 5 green

together

Name ___

2 purple and 2 red

together

Name ___

0 green and 2 black

together

Name ___

2 brown and 1 yellow

together

Name ___

3 blue and 3 green

together

Name ___

5 brown and 0 red

together

Name ___

1 yellow and 9 black

together

Name

Name

Name

Name

Name

Name

0 red and 5 purple

together

1 green and 6 brown

together

2 orange and 6 brown

together

1 orange and 7 black

together

4 orange and 6 purple

together

5 green and 5 red

together

Name _____

8 green and 2 orange

together

Name _____

2 yellow and 7 purple

together

Name _____

10 yellow and 0 blue

together

Name _____

4 orange and 2 red

together

Name _____

1 green and 6 blue

together

Name _____

5 purple and 3 brown

together

Name

7 brown and 1 orange

together

Name

1 red and 5 yellow

together

Name

10 blue and 0 black

together

Name

8 purple and 1 blue

together

Name

1 yellow and 8 orange

together

Name

6 red and 3 brown

together

Name _____

2 green and 3 black

together

Name _____

3 blue and 6 yellow

together

Name _____

4 brown and 4 purple

together

Name _____

5 purple and 2 yellow

together

Name _____

3 green and 5 black

together

Name _____

8 black and 2 brown

together

Name _____

7 purple and 3 blue

together

Name _____

3 brown and 3 yellow

together

Name _____

7 yellow and 2 red

together

Name _____

1 black and 4 purple

together

Name _____

4 red and 6 green

together

Name _____

6 green and 2 yellow

together

Name _____

4 yellow and 4 orange

together

Name _____

3 red and 4 orange

together

Name _____

8 purple and 2 black

together

Name _____

2 orange and 4 blue

together

Name _____

6 blue and 1 black

together

Name _____

4 brown and 1 green

together

Name _____

1 purple and 5 green

together

Name _____

1 black and 1 orange

together

Name _____

3 yellow and 4 brown

together

Name _____

7 blue and 3 yellow

together

Name _____

1 orange and 5 purple

together

Name _____

2 orange and 4 red

together

Name _____

7 yellow and 1 green

together

Name _____

3 black and 6 orange

together

Name _____

4 blue and 2 red

together

Name _____

5 purple and 4 green

together

Name _____

1 brown and 9 blue

together

Name _____

6 brown and 1 orange

together

Name _____

2 orange and 3 yellow

together

Name _____

5 green and 4 blue

together

Name _____

3 brown and 7 red

together

Name _____

5 blue and 2 purple

together

Name _____

1 brown and 8 green

together

Name _____

0 yellow and 4 red

together

Name _____

6 yellow and 2 green

together

Name _____

4 green and 3 purple

together

Name _____

7 purple and 2 orange

together

Name _____

5 orange and 4 blue

together

Name _____

2 red and 4 black

together

Name _____

3 black and 1 purple

together

Name _____

6 purple and 4 yellow

together

Name _____

9 blue and 1 orange

together

Name _____

5 yellow and 3 brown

together

Name _____

0 brown and 3 black

together

Name _____

8 red and 1 brown

together

Name _____

1 black and 2 red

together

Name _____

5 brown and 3 orange

together

Name _____

4 purple and 3 blue

together

Name _____

0 black and 7 green

together

Name _____

3 brown and 2 purple

together

Name _____

5 red and 5 blue

together

Name _____

2 blue and 6 red

together

Name _____

3 blue and 0 purple

together ☐

Name _____

6 black and 3 yellow

together ☐

Name _____

0 black and 6 blue

together ☐

Name _____

2 red and 3 orange

together ☐

Name _____

8 green and 1 yellow

together ☐

Name _____

3 brown and 6 blue

together ☐

Solving Horizontal and Vertical Number Sentences Using a Color-Word Key

Here are two ways children have completed the exercises in this section.

Name **Martha**

R B
B R
R B
. R
R

5 red
+ 3 blue
―――――
8

together

© 2004 bby Publications 502-633-9400

Name **Ned**

P P P P
Y Y Y Y

$4 + 4 = 8$

purple   yellow

together

position on page ▶						
page 41	5	8	9	8	5	10
page 42	7	5	10	7	8	7
page 43	9	9	10	10	9	10
page 44	6	8	5	8	10	10
page 45	8	7	6	10	10	8
page 46	9	9	9	8	9	10
page 47	6	6	7	10	6	2
page 48	6	10	4	9	9	5
page 49	7	9	8	10	3	3
page 50	10	6	9	3	9	5
page 51	9	5	5	9	8	4
page 52	9	5	5	10	9	4
page 53	10	8	4	5	8	10
page 54	3	6	10	5	4	8
page 55	2	3	6	10	9	7
page 56	10	9	7	8	10	5
page 57	8	7	8	10	6	5
page 58	7	8	6	9	9	7
page 59	10	7	8	9	9	4
page 60	6	7	8	7	5	10

Name

$4 + 5 =$

green   brown

together

8 blue
$+ 2$ green

together

Name

$4 + 4 =$

purple   yellow

together

Name

4 black
$+ 1$ blue

together

Name

$2 + 3 =$

green   black

together

Name

5 red
$+ 3$ blue

together

Name _____

$9 + 1 =$

green   red

together

Name _____

$3 + 2 =$

brown   red

together

Name _____

$5 + 2 =$

red   black

together

---

2 purple
$+ 5$ brown

together

---

4 brown
$+ 4$ black

together

---

3 orange
$+ 4$ green

together

© 2004 bby Publications 502-633-9400

Name

2 + 8 = ☐ together

purple   green

Name

7 + 2 = ☐ together

red   yellow

Name

6 + 3 = ☐ together

yellow   blue

Name

6 black
+ 4 brown
_____
☐ together

Name

2 black
+ 7 orange
_____
☐ together

Name

7 blue
+ 3 brown
_____
☐ together

Name _____

$0 + 5 =$ ☐

red   purple

together

Name _____

$3 + 5 =$ ☐

orange   green

together

Name _____

$5 + 1 =$ ☐

yellow   red

together

Name _____

$\begin{array}{r} 5 \text{ green} \\ + 5 \text{ red} \\ \hline \end{array}$ ☐

together

Name _____

$\begin{array}{r} 4 \text{ orange} \\ + 6 \text{ purple} \\ \hline \end{array}$ ☐

together

Name _____

$\begin{array}{r} 2 \text{ orange} \\ + 6 \text{ brown} \\ \hline \end{array}$ ☐

together

44   bby Practice Pages: **Beginning Addition 0-10**

Name _____

$3 + 3 =$

brown   yellow

together

Name _____

$1 + 6 =$

green   brown

together

Name _____

$1 + 7 =$

orange   black

together

Name _____

6 green
$+ 2$ yellow

together

Name _____

4 red
$+ 6$ green

together

Name _____

7 purple
$+ 3$ blue

together

Name _____

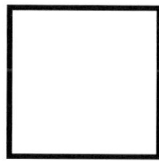

8 + 1 =

purple   blue

together

Name _____

1 0 blue

+ 0 black

together

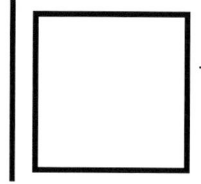

Name _____

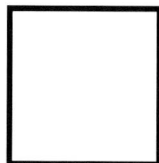

6 + 3 =

red   brown

together

Name _____

1 yellow

+ 8 orange

together

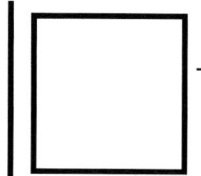

Name _____

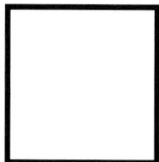

7 + 2 =

yellow   red

together

Name _____

7 brown

+ 1 orange

together

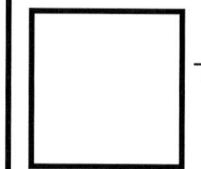

Name _____

$3 + 4 =$

yellow   brown

together

Name _____

$2 + 4 =$

orange   red

together

Name _____

$1 + 5 =$

red   yellow

together

Name _____

$\begin{array}{r} 1 \text{ black} \\ + 1 \text{ orange} \\ \hline \end{array}$

together

Name _____

$\begin{array}{r} 1 \text{ purple} \\ + 5 \text{ green} \\ \hline \end{array}$

together

Name _____

$\begin{array}{r} 7 \text{ blue} \\ + 3 \text{ yellow} \\ \hline \end{array}$

together

Name _____

$0 + 4 =$

yellow   red   together

Name _____

$3 + 7 =$

brown   red   together

Name _____

$1 + 5 =$

orange   purple   together

Name _____

2 orange
$+ 3$ yellow

together

Name _____

1 brown
$+ 8$ green

together

Name _____

5 green
$+ 4$ blue

together

Name _____

5 + 3 = ☐
yellow   brown   together

8 + 1 = ☐
red   brown   together

5 + 2 = ☐
blue   purple   together

Name _____

0 brown
$+ 3$ black
_____
☐ together

1 black
$+ 2$ red
_____
☐ together

6 purple
$+ 4$ yellow
_____
☐ together

Name

6 + 3 = [ ]
black   yellow
together

Name

2 red
+ 3 orange
together

Name

0 + 6 = [ ]
black   blue
together

Name

8 green
+ 1 yellow
together

Name

9 + 1 = [ ]
blue   orange
together

Name

3 blue
+ 0 purple
together

Name ___

4 + 1 =

purple   red   together

Name ___

2 + 3 =

green   black   together

Name ___

3 + 6 =

brown   blue   together

Name ___

3 yellow
+ 1 black
together

Name ___

3 yellow
+ 5 orange
together

Name ___

6 orange
+ 3 green
together

Name _____

1 + 4 =

purple   orange

together

purple

Name _____

2 blue
+ 2 purple

together

Name _____

2 + 3 =

blue   brown

together

Name _____

0 green
+ 9 blue

together

Name _____

4 + 5 =

red   purple

together

Name _____

2 black
+ 8 red

together

Name _____

1 + 3 =
orange   brown   together

3 + 5 =
red   green   together

4 + 6 =
blue   orange   together

Name _____

3 black
+ 7 yellow
together

1 red
+ 7 blue
together

4 green
+ 1 black
together

Name _____

$1 + 9 =$ ⬜ together

yellow black

Name _____

$3 + 3 =$ ⬜ together

blue green

Name _____

$2 + 1 =$ ⬜ together

yellow purple

Name _____

5 purple
$+ 3$ brown

⬜ together

Name _____

2 purple
$+ 2$ red

⬜ together

Name _____

5 brown
$+ 0$ red

⬜ together

Name _____

$$4 + 2 = \boxed{}$$

orange   red

together

Name _____

$$2 + 1 = \boxed{}$$

brown   yellow

together

Name _____

$$0 + 2 = \boxed{}$$

green   black

together

Name _____

$$\begin{array}{r} 1 \text{ green} \\ + 6 \text{ blue} \\ \hline \end{array} \quad \boxed{}$$

together

Name _____

$$\begin{array}{r} 7 \text{ yellow} \\ + 2 \text{ purple} \\ \hline \end{array} \quad \boxed{}$$

together

Name _____

$$\begin{array}{r} 8 \text{ green} \\ + 2 \text{ orange} \\ \hline \end{array} \quad \boxed{}$$

together

Name _____

© 2004 bby Publications 502-633-9400

5 + 2 =

purple   yellow

together

Name _____

© 2004 bby Publications 502-633-9400

3 + 6 =

blue   yellow

together

Name _____

© 2004 bby Publications 502-633-9400

10 + 0 =

yellow   blue

together

Name _____

2 green
+ 3 black

together

Name _____

8 black
+ 2 brown

together

Name _____

4 brown
+ 4 purple

together

© 2004 bby Publications • All Rights Reserved • bby Practice Pages: **Beginning Addition 0-10**

Name

$4 + 4 =$

yellow   orange   together

Name

$3 + 4 =$

red   orange   together

Name

$3 + 5 =$

green   black   together

Name

4 brown
+ 1 green

together

Name

2 orange
+ 4 blue

together

Name

8 purple
+ 2 black

together

$4 + 2 = \square$

blue   red   together

$7 + 1 = \square$

yellow   green   together

$6 + 1 = \square$

blue   black   together

---

6 brown
$+ 1$ orange

together

---

5 purple
$+ 4$ green

together

---

3 black
$+ 6$ orange

together

Name _____

$6 + 2 =$

yellow green together

Name _____

$4 + 3 =$

green purple together

Name _____

$1 + 9 =$

brown blue together

Name _____

3 black
$+ 1$ purple

together

Name _____

5 orange
$+ 4$ blue

together

Name _____

7 purple
$+ 2$ orange

together

Name _____

$5 + 3 =$

brown   orange   together

Name _____

$4 + 3 =$

purple   blue   together

Name _____

$2 + 4 =$

red   black   together

Name _____

$$\begin{array}{r} 5 \text{ red} \\ + 5 \text{ blue} \\ \hline \end{array}$$

together

Name _____

$$\begin{array}{r} 3 \text{ brown} \\ + 2 \text{ purple} \\ \hline \end{array}$$

together

Name _____

$$\begin{array}{r} 0 \text{ black} \\ + 7 \text{ green} \\ \hline \end{array}$$

together

Writing and Solving Horizontal and Vertical Number Sentences Using a Shape Key

The exercises in this section provide opportunities for young learners to write addition number sentences by counting the number of shapes in a subset and writing the sum of the set of combined shapes. Children will make connections between the number of squares containing shapes and the sum. They will begin to estimate by making judgments such as "I see two shapes being used, but I still see some empty squares, so I know the sum is less than 10. The only time I write 10 is when the whole grid is filled."

Here are two ways children have completed the exercises in this section.

Name **Debra**

$3 + 4 = 7$ shapes

© 2004 bby Publications 502-633-9400

Name **Elizabeth**

$$0 + 8 = 8$$ shapes

© 2004 bby Publications 502-633-9400

position on page ►						
page 61	$3+4=7$	$6+1=7$	$4+1=5$	$2+2=4$	$3+7=10$	$0+8=8$
page 62	$6+1=7$	$2+7=9$	$1+4=5$	$3+6=9$	$5+2=7$	$6+2=8$
page 63	$4+3=7$	$0+6=6$	$1+8=9$	$3+1=4$	$5+3=8$	$1+1=2$
page 64	$1+8=9$	$2+5=7$	$6+3=9$	$7+1=8$	$2+1=3$	$6+3=9$
page 65	$9+1=10$	$3+3=6$	$1+5=6$	$0+9=9$	$6+4=10$	$3+0=3$
page 66	$0+7=7$	$2+3=5$	$1+3=4$	$8+2=10$	$1+5=6$	$0+3=3$
page 67	$7+0=7$	$4+4=8$	$1+9=10$	$5+0=5$	$4+5=9$	$2+6=8$
page 68	$3+6=9$	$9+0=9$	$4+0=4$	$4+6=10$	$1+2=3$	$7+1=8$
page 69	$0+5=5$	$4+2=6$	$5+4=9$	$2+0=2$	$7+3=10$	$2+4=6$
page 70	$2+3=5$	$8+0=8$	$5+5=10$	$10+0=10$	$2+7=9$	$8+2=10$
page 71	$4+1=5$	$0+8=8$	$5+4=9$	$10+0=10$	$5+3=8$	$6+1=7$
page 72	$4+0=4$	$6+2=8$	$9+1=10$	$2+1=3$	$6+4=10$	$2+7=9$
page 73	$1+8=9$	$1+1=2$	$1+8=9$	$1+5=6$	$4+5=9$	$0+6=6$
page 74	$1+4=5$	$2+4=6$	$5+5=10$	$3+7=10$	$5+2=7$	$4+4=8$
page 75	$7+0=7$	$8+2=10$	$0+7=7$	$8+2=10$	$4+6=10$	$8+0=8$
page 76	$1+5=6$	$2+6=8$	$6+3=9$	$5+0=5$	$0+9=9$	$2+3=5$
page 77	$3+4=7$	$0+3=3$	$0+5=5$	$1+2=3$	$7+3=10$	$3+3=6$
page 78	$3+6=9$	$6+3=9$	$1+9=10$	$2+7=9$	$2+2=4$	$4+2=6$
page 79	$1+3=4$	$3+0=3$	$4+3=7$	$3+6=9$	$3+1=4$	$2+5=7$
page 80	$6+1=7$	$7+1=8$	$2+3=5$	$7+1=8$	$2+0=2$	$9+0=9$

© 2004 bby Publications • All Rights Reserved • bby Practice Pages: **Beginning Addition 0-10**

Name

shapes

© 2004 bby Publications 502-633-9400

Name

shapes

© 2004 bby Publications 502-633-9400

Name

shapes

© 2004 bby Publications 502-633-9400

Name

shapes

© 2004 bby Publications 502-633-9400

Name

shapes

© 2004 bby Publications 502-633-9400

Name

shapes

bby Practice Pages: **Beginning Addition 0-10**

© 2004 bby Publications 502-633-9400

Name _____

shapes

□ = □ + □

●

◀

© 2004 bby Publications 502-633-9400

Name _____

shapes

□ = □ + □

◀

●

© 2004 bby Publications 502-633-9400

Name _____

shapes

□ = □ + □

●

◀

© 2004 bby Publications 502-633-9400

Name _____

shapes

□ □ + □

● ◀

© 2004 bby Publications 502-633-9400

Name _____

shapes

□ □ + □

◀ ●

© 2004 bby Publications 502-633-9400

Name _____

shapes

□ □ + □

◀ ●

Name

shapes

+ =

Name

shapes

+ =

Name

shapes

+ =

Name

shapes

+

Name

shapes

+

Name

shapes

+

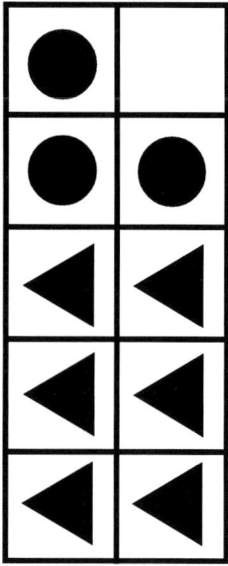

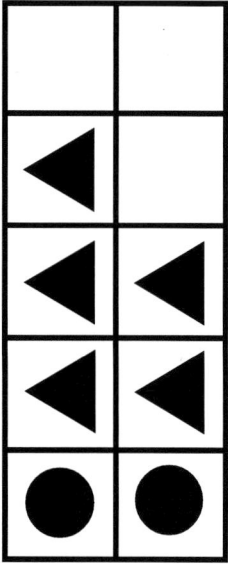

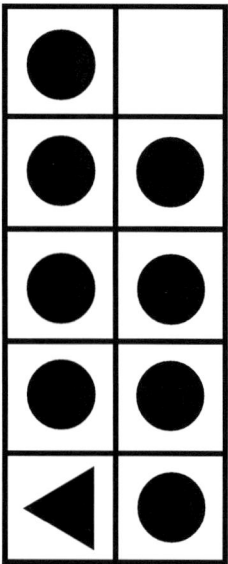

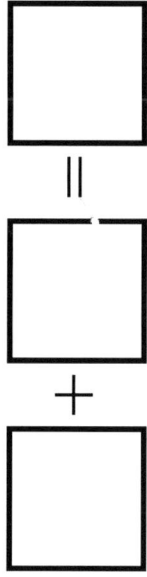

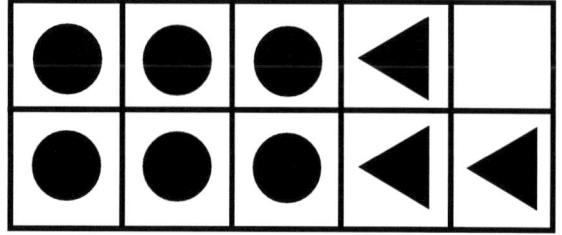

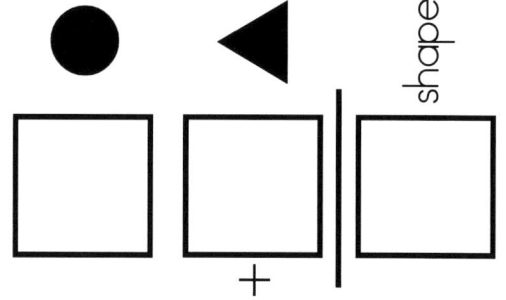

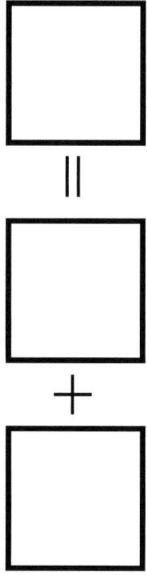

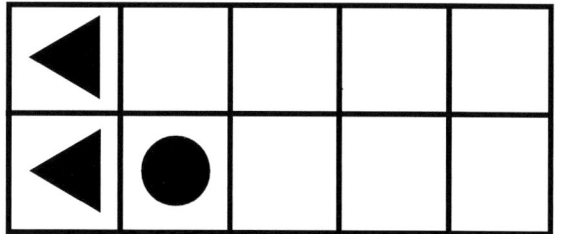

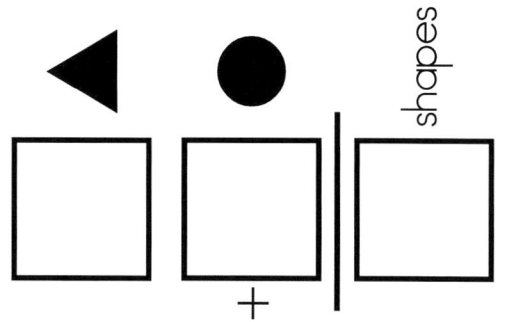

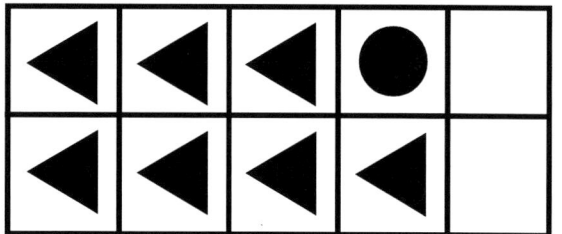

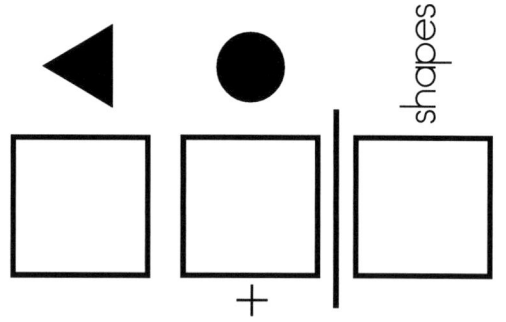

Name

shapes

＋

＝

Name

shapes

＋

Name

shapes

＋

＝

Name

shapes

＋

Name

shapes

＋

＝

Name

shapes

＋

Name

shapes

+ =

Name

shapes

+ =

Name

shapes

+ =

Name

shapes

+

Name

shapes

+

Name

shapes

+

Name

shapes

+

=

Name

shapes

+

Name

shapes

+

=

Name

shapes

+

Name

shapes

+

=

Name

shapes

+

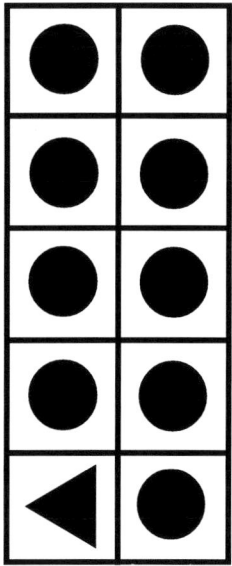

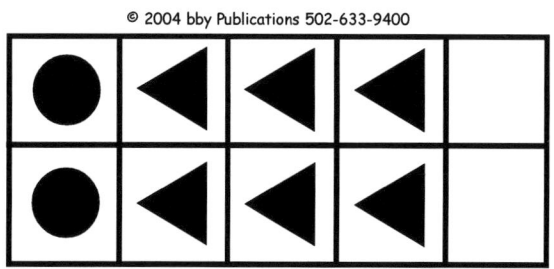

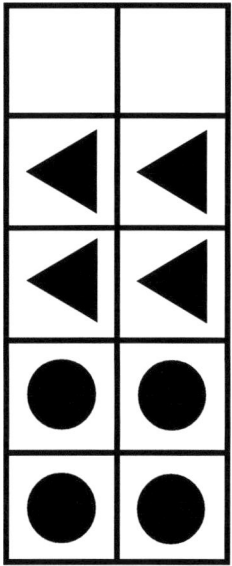

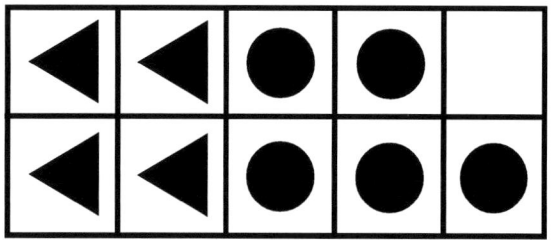

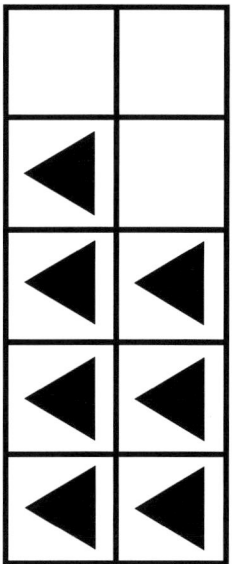

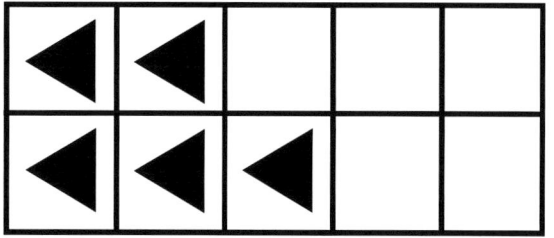

Name _____

shapes

$+$

$=$

Name _____

shapes

$+$

Name _____

shapes

$+$

$=$

Name _____

shapes

$+$

Name _____

shapes

$+$

$=$

Name _____

shapes

$+$

Name

Name

Name

Name

Name

Name

shapes

shapes

shapes

shapes

shapes

shapes

+

+

+

+

=

=

=

© 2004 bby Publications 502-633-9400

© 2004 bby Publications 502-633-9400

© 2004 bby Publications 502-633-9400

© 2004 bby Publications 502-633-9400

© 2004 bby Publications 502-633-9400

© 2004 bby Publications 502-633-9400

Name _____

shapes

Name _____

shapes

Name _____

shapes

Name _____

shapes

Name _____

shapes

Name _____

shapes

Name ___

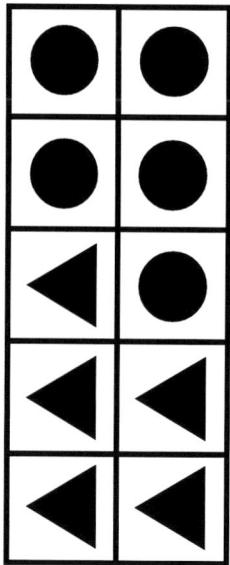

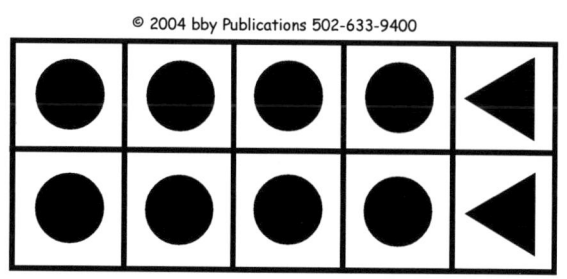

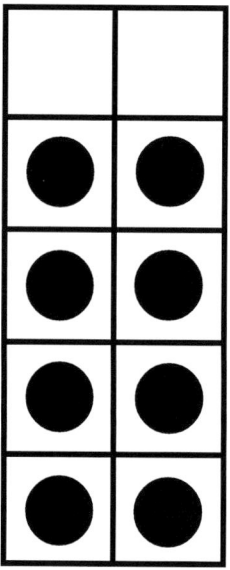

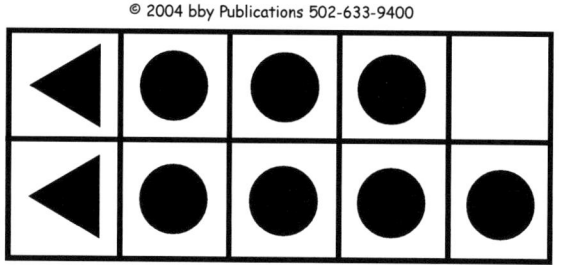

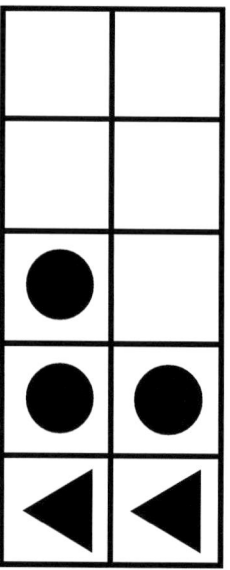

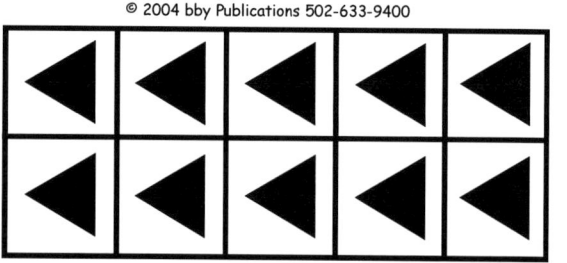

shapes

Name ___

shapes

Name ___

shapes

Name ___

shapes

Name ___

shapes

Name ___

shapes

Name__________

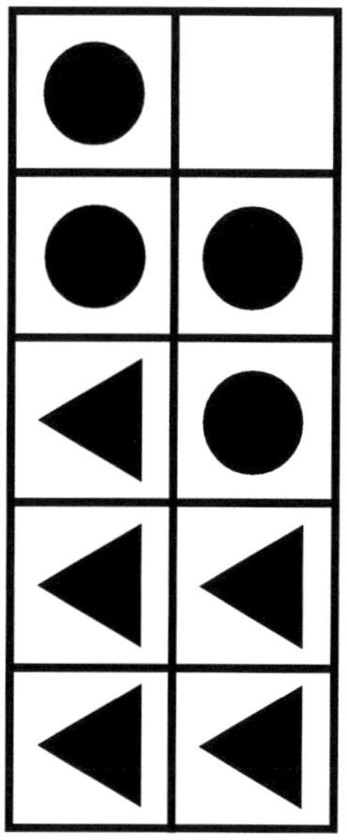

□ + □ = □ shapes

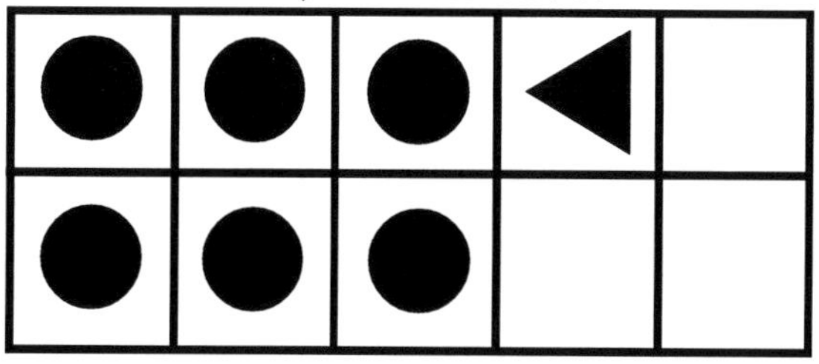

Name__________

□ + □ = □ shapes

Name__________

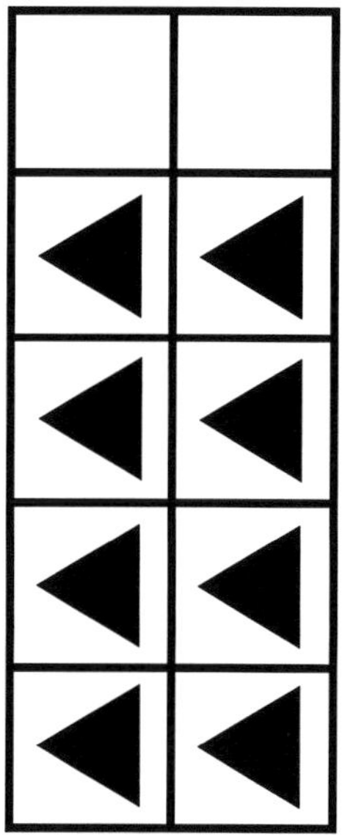

□ + □ = □ shapes

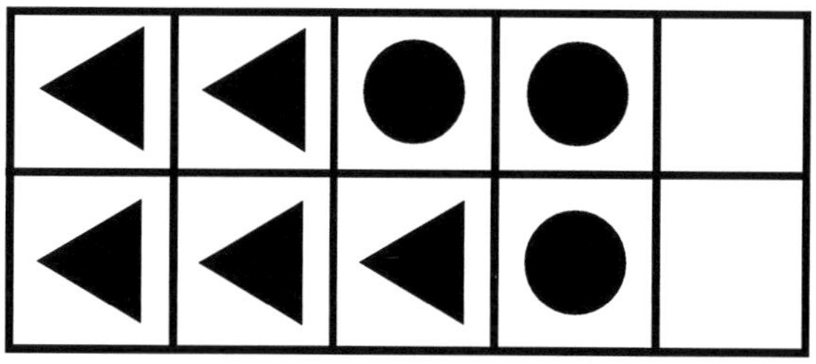

Name__________

□ + □ = □ shapes

Name__________

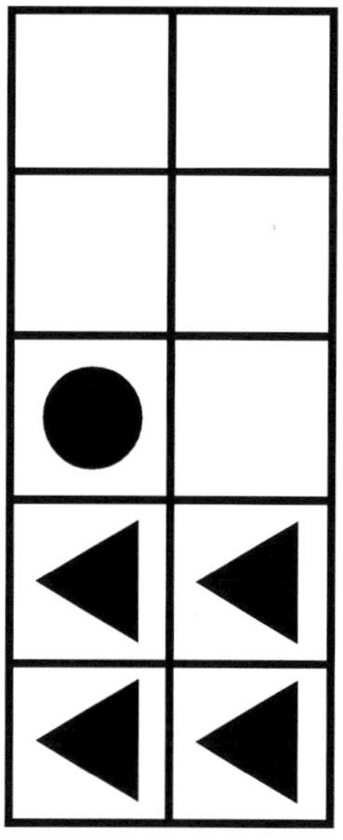

□ + □ = □ shapes

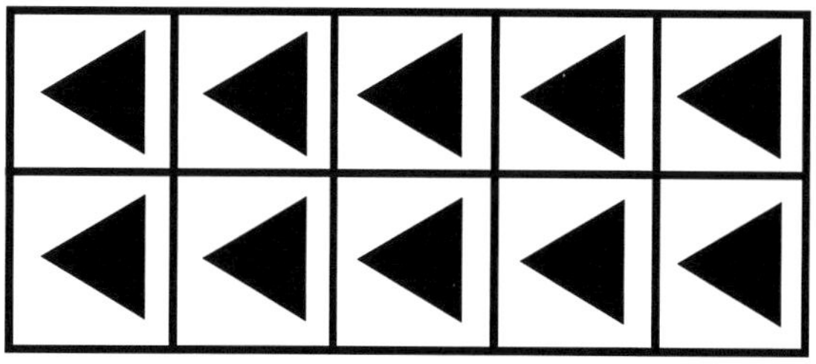

Name__________

□ + □ = □ shapes

Name _____

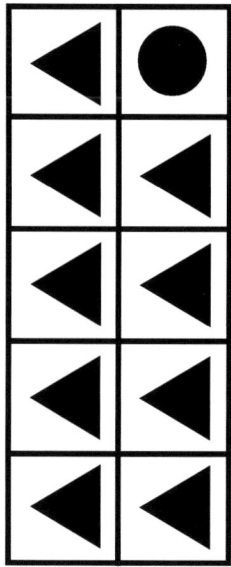

☐ + ☐ = ☐ shapes

Name _____

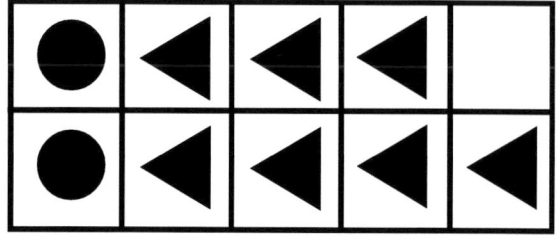

☐ + ☐ = ☐ shapes

Name _____

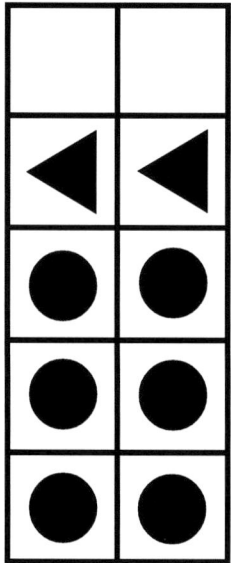

☐ + ☐ = ☐ shapes

Name _____

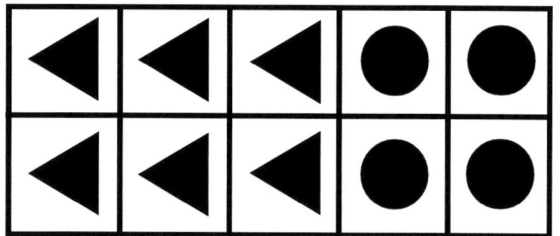

☐ + ☐ | ☐ shapes

Name _____

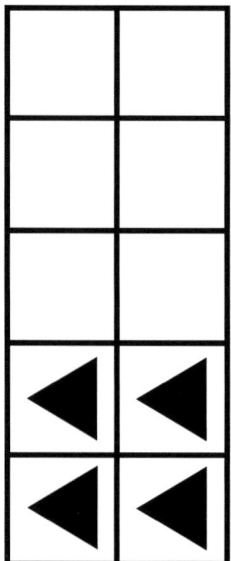

☐ + ☐ | ☐ shapes

Name _____

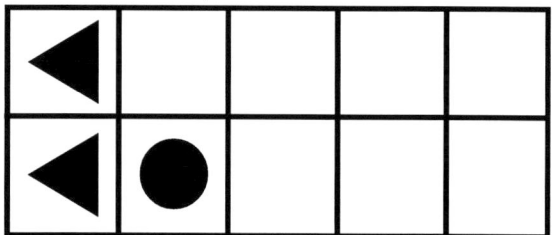

☐ + ☐ | ☐ shapes

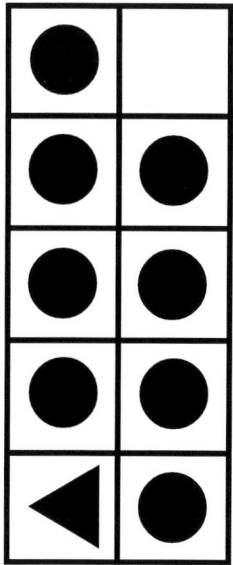

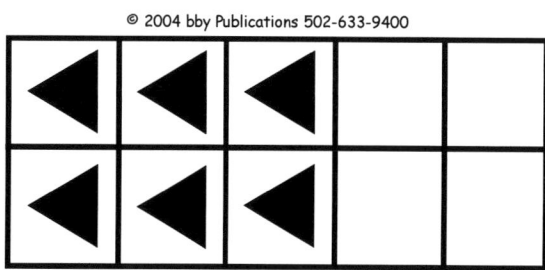

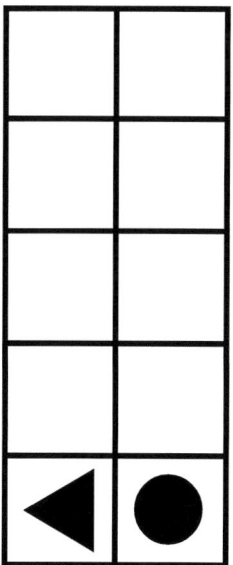

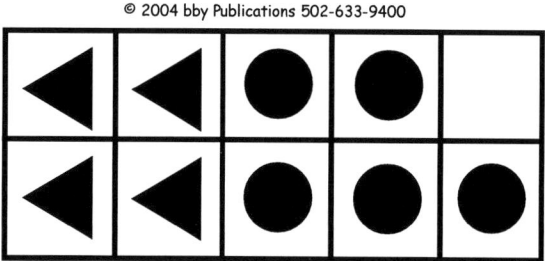

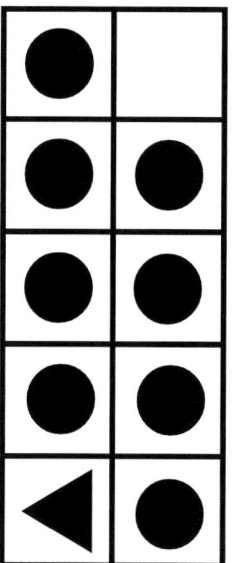

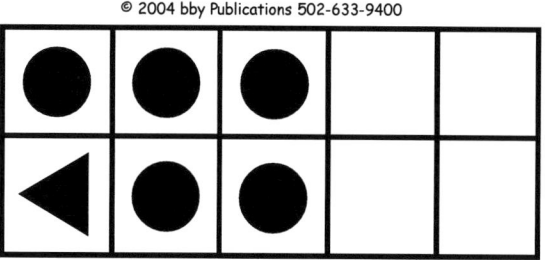

© 2004 bby Publications 502-633-9400

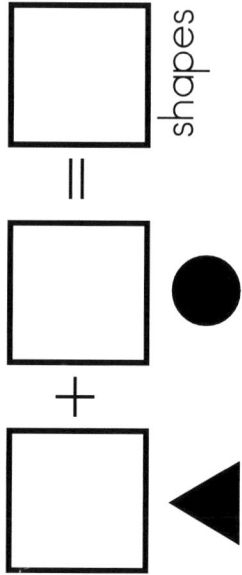

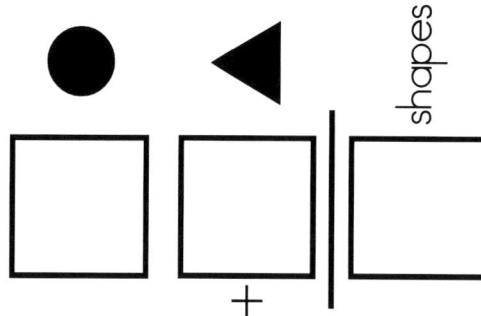

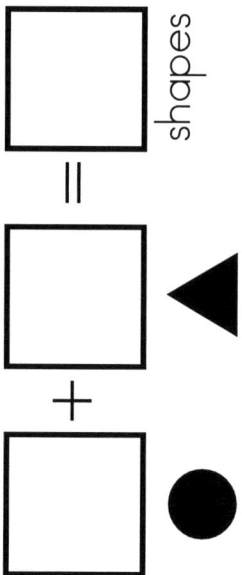

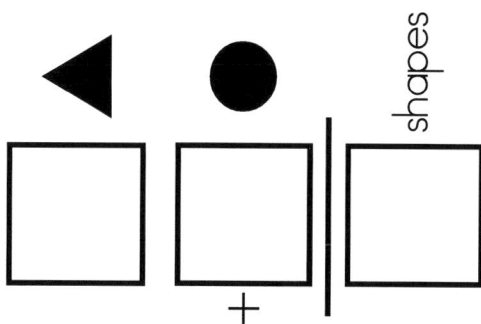

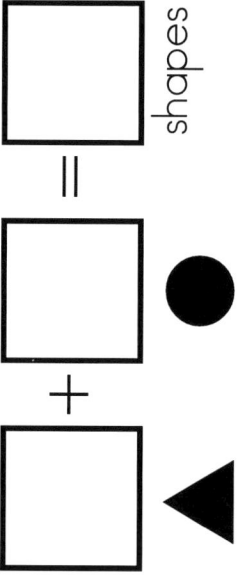

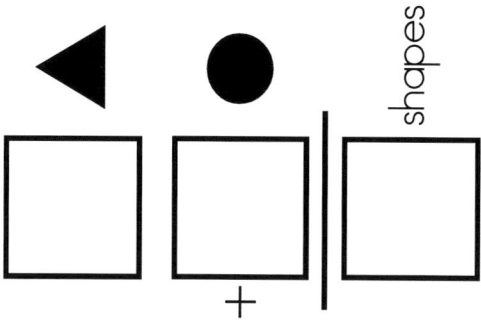

Name

shapes

© 2004 bby Publications 502-633-9400

Name

shapes

Name

shapes

© 2004 bby Publications 502-633-9400

Name

shapes

© 2004 bby Publications 502-633-9400

Name

shapes

© 2004 bby Publications 502-633-9400

Name

shapes

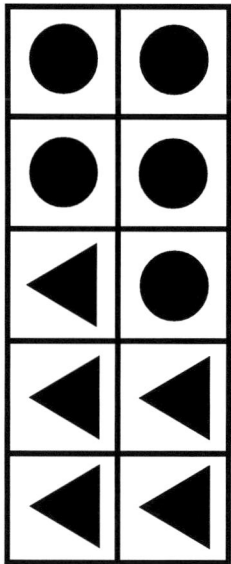

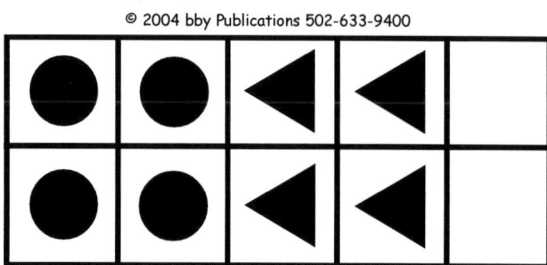

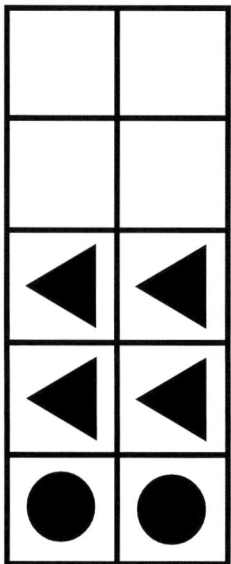

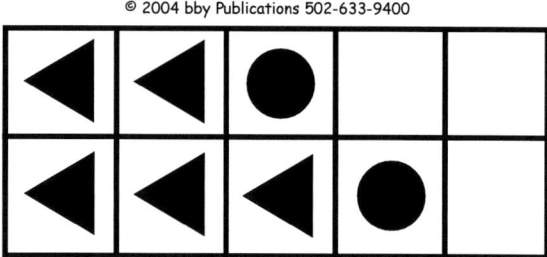

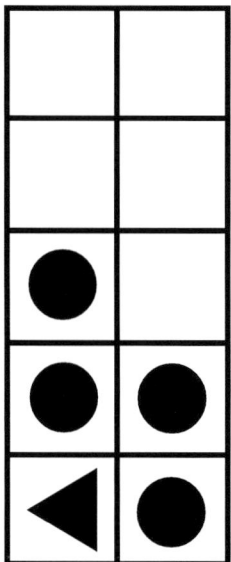

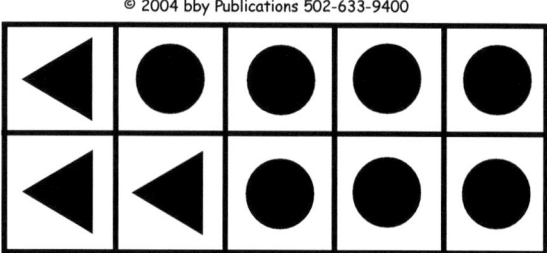

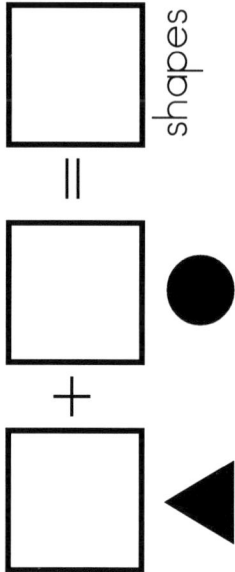

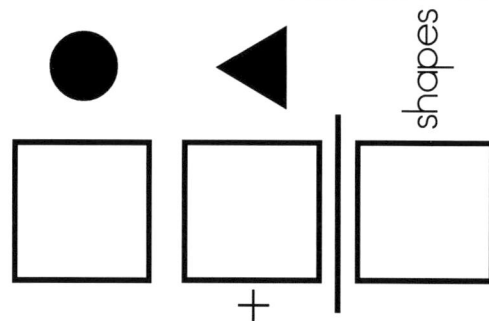

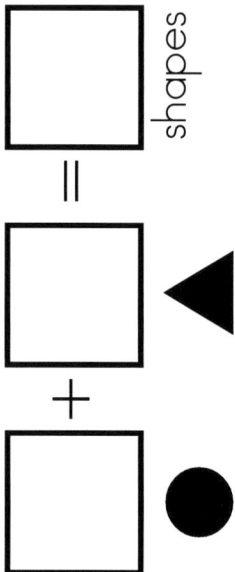

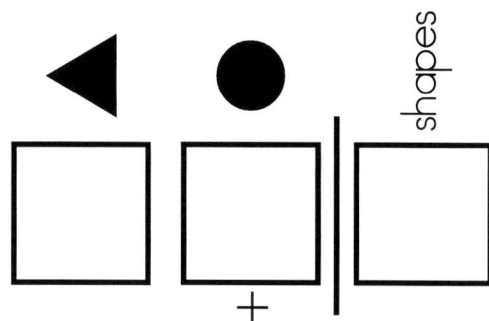

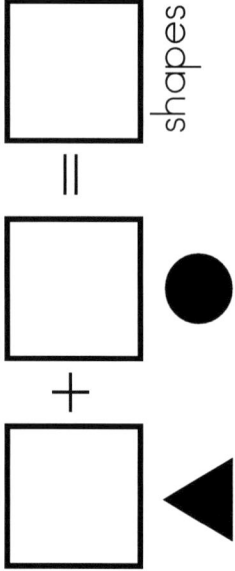

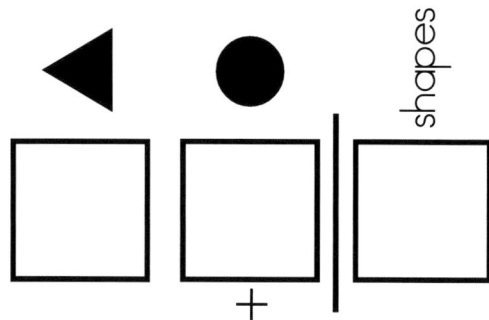

Name

Name

Name

Name

Name

Name

shapes

shapes

shapes

shapes

shapes

shapes

74

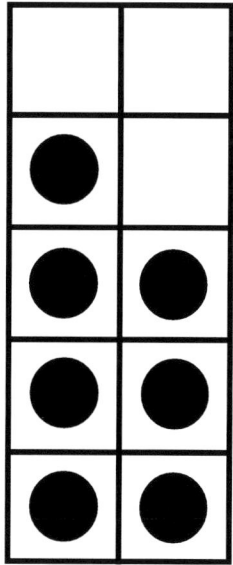

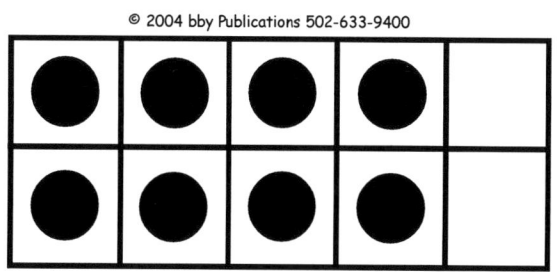

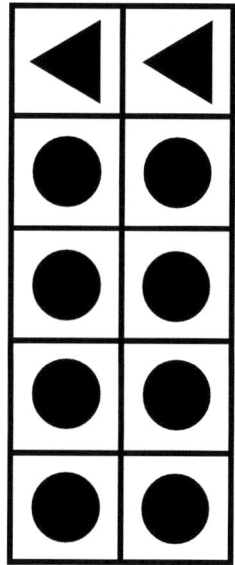

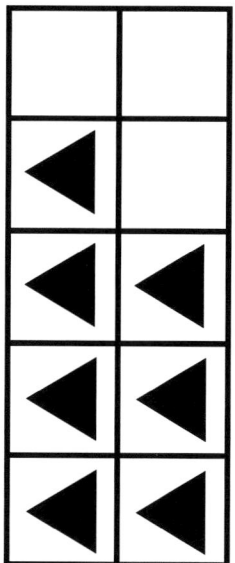

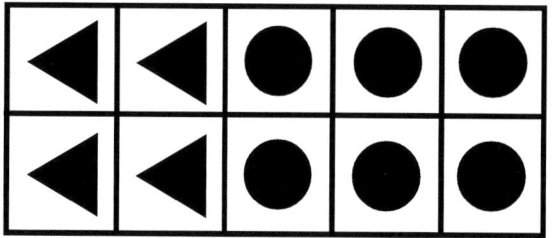

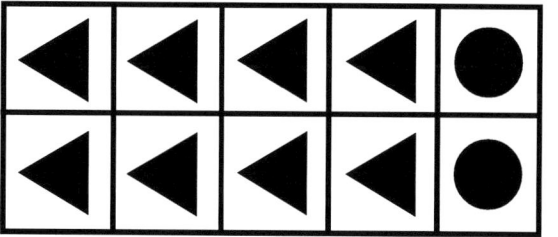

Name _____

□ = shapes

□ ⚫

+

□ ◀

Name _____

□ = shapes

□ ◀

+

□ ⚫

Name _____

□ = shapes

□ ⚫

+

□ ◀

Name _____

⚫ ◀

□ □ | □

+ shapes

Name _____

◀ ⚫

□ □ | □

+ shapes

Name _____

◀ ⚫

□ □ | □

+ shapes

shapes

shapes

Name

shapes

Name

Name

shapes

Name

shapes

Name

shapes

Name

Name _____

shapes

=

+

Name _____

shapes

+

Name _____

shapes

=

+

Name _____

shapes

+

Name _____

shapes

=

+

Name _____

shapes

+

Name _____

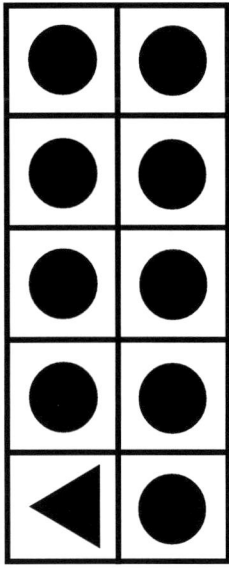

shapes

Name _____

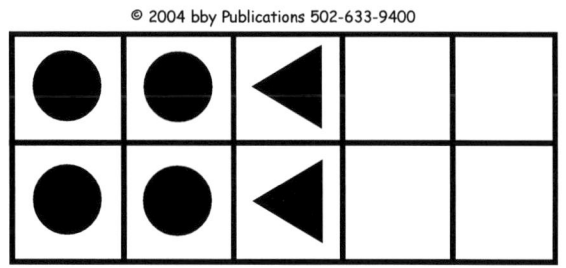

shapes

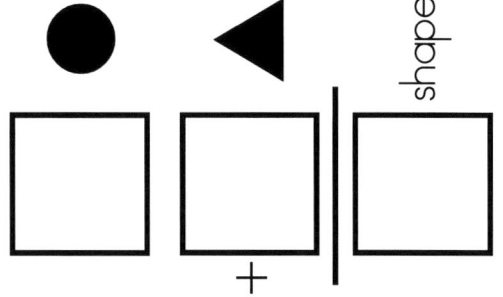

Name _____

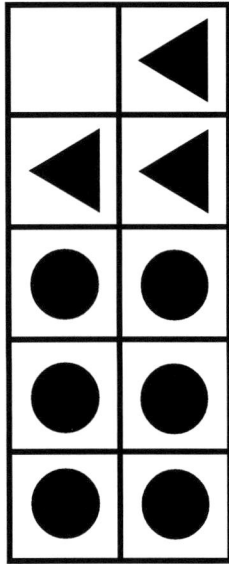

shapes

Name _____

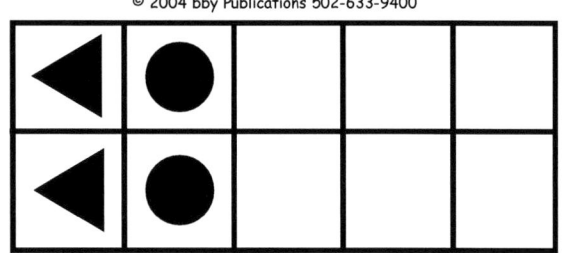

shapes

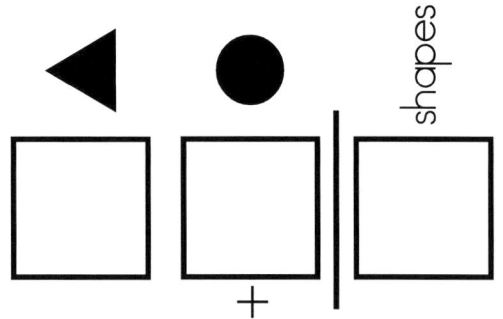

Name _____

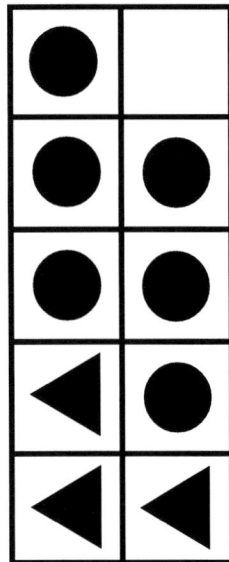
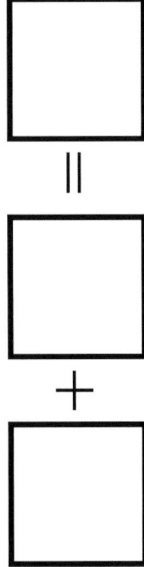

shapes

Name _____

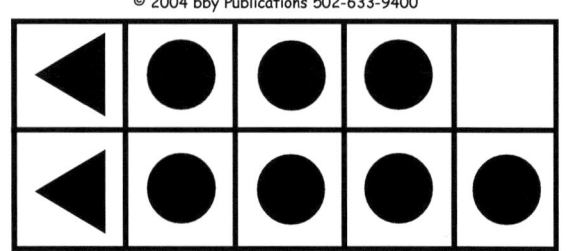

shapes

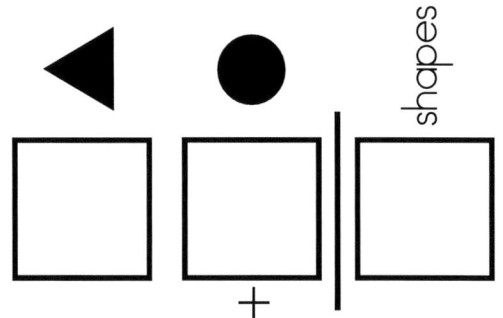

© 2004 bby Publications 502-633-9400

Name

shapes

© 2004 bby Publications 502-633-9400

Name

shapes

+ =

Name

shapes

© 2004 bby Publications 502-633-9400

+ =

Name

shapes

© 2004 bby Publications 502-633-9400

Name

shapes

+ =

Name

shapes

+

Name

shapes

=

+

Name

shapes

=

+

Name

shapes

=

+

Name

shapes

+

Name

shapes

+

Name

shapes

+

Other Related bby Products

bby Practice Pages

- Counting Mixed Coins
- Modeling Numbers 0-100
- Choosing Coins
- Addition Facts 0-10
- Subtraction Facts 0-10
- Numbers and Words 0-10
- Making Ten
- Beginning Addition 0-10
- Numbers and Words 11-20
- Addition Facts 11-20
- Subtraction Facts 11-20
- Making Change Through $1.00

Practice Pages coming soon in 2005

- Beginning Subtraction 0-10
- Double-digit Addition Through 100
- Double-digit Subtraction through 100
- Modeling Fractions
- Modeling Mixed Numbers and Improper Fractions
- Beginning Decimals, Fractions, and Percents
- Addition and Subtraction Word Problems Through 10
- Addition and Subtraction Word Problems Through 20
- Addition and Subtraction Word Problems Through 100
- Converting Fractions to Decimals and Percents
- Multiple Addends: Sums Through 20
- Equivalent Equations: Addition and Subtraction 0-20

bby Crayon Wipe-off Mats

Finally, for the first time teachers can stop wasting money on expensive dry-erase markers that end up causing more trouble than they are worth. bby is proud to present our seven sets of CRAYON wipe-off mats designed to take the hassle out of hands-on teaching.

Any regular, dark-colored crayon used on our special mats will mark and wipe-off with ease. Students can write equations, create graphs and tables, work with time and money, learn number sense standards, use multiplication tables, work on addition, subtraction, symmetry…the possibilities are endless depending on the selected mat. When students are finished with one idea and wish to start with a blank slate, a dry, paper towel wipes the crayon off.

Each set of mats has an introductory side and an advanced side to work with every child's individual needs. The sets are packaged in quantities of 25, with 24 student mats (8 1/2 X 11) and 1 teacher mat (11 X 17).

- Mat Set #1: Ten-grid / Twenty-grid
- Mat Set #2: Hundred-grid / Blank
- Mat Set #3: 1 cm. / 2 cm. Grids
- Mat Set #4: 1 cm. / 2 cm. Dots
- Mat Set #5: Hundred-chart / Multiplication Table
- Mat Set #6: Introductory Coins / Advanced Coins
- Mat Set #7: Introductory Clocks / Advanced Clocks